OSCAR the Mouse and friends

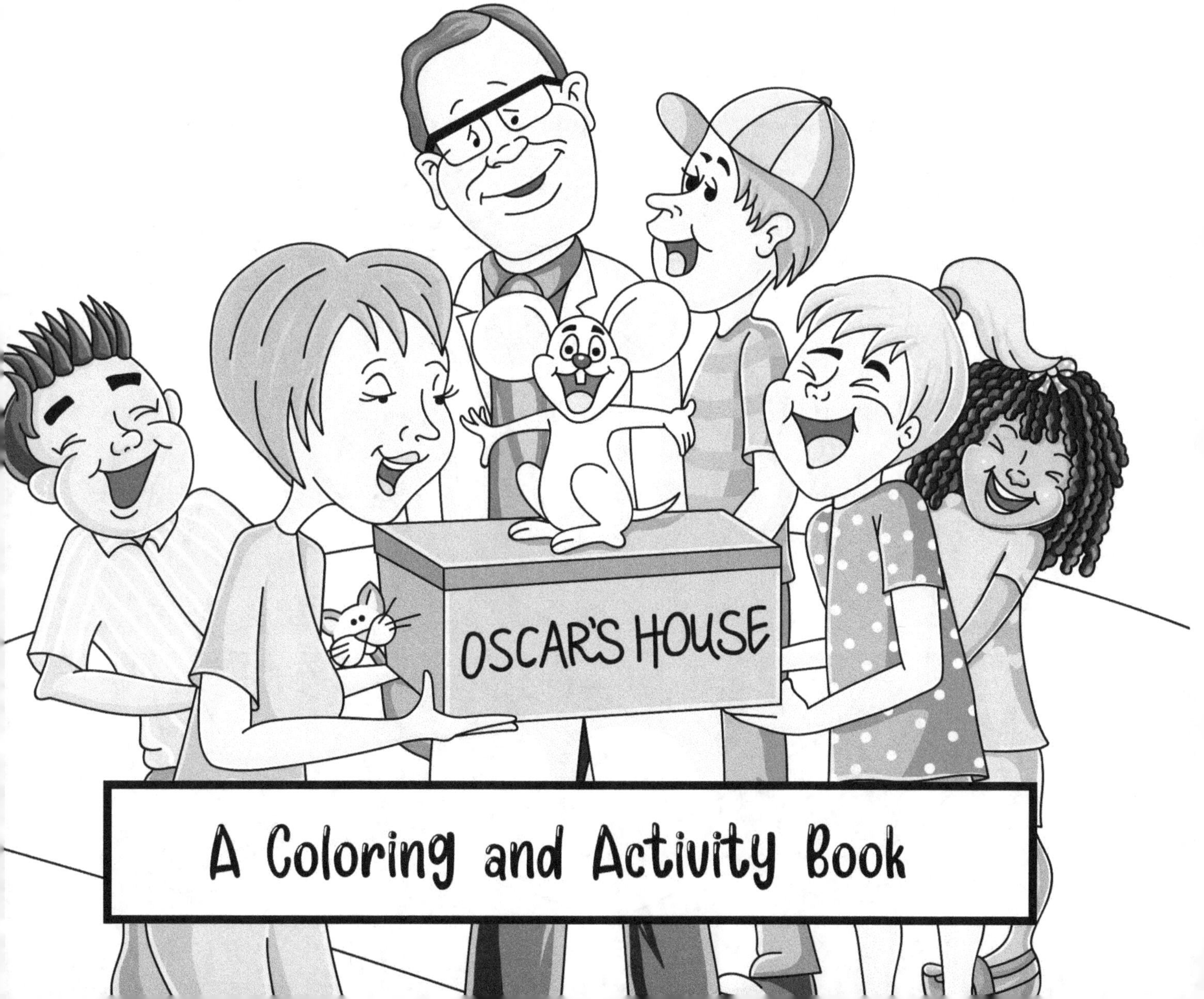

OSCAR'S HOUSE

A Coloring and Activity Book

Draw a line on the road from Oscar to his cheese.

A E I O U are all vowels
Circle and say them.
Then say all the letters in order.

Join the numbers from 1 to 10

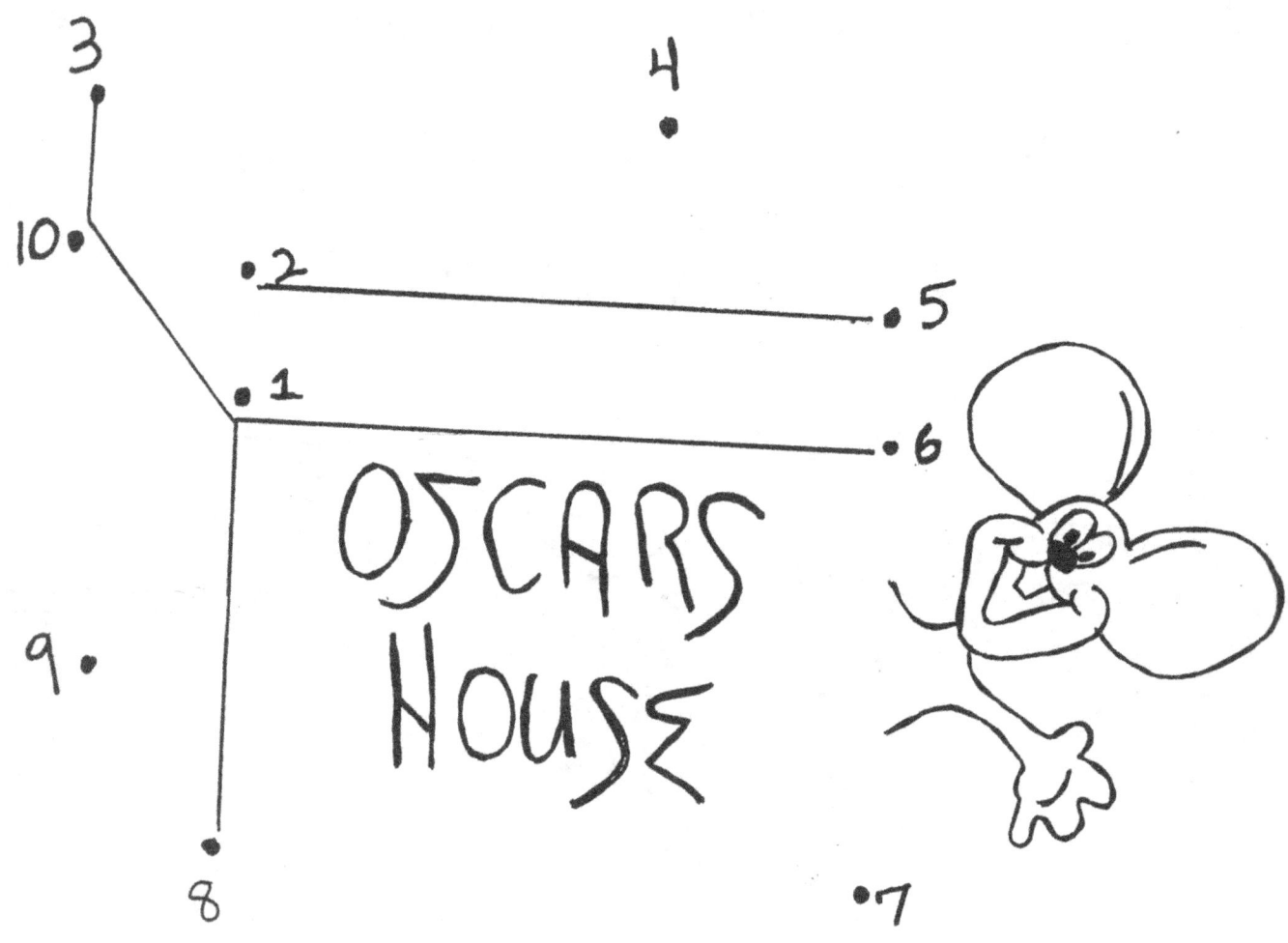

You can do it!

Smiles are always Good!

You make me smile!

Draw a line from each word to a picture that names each of Oscar's friends.

Mom .

Uncle Oscar .

Mimi .

Brother Paul .

Javier .

Keisha .

Use the letters to spell what each picture is.

1. P L A M _____   2. D B E _____

3. A H T _____   4. U N R _____

Color as shown

How many are on each plate

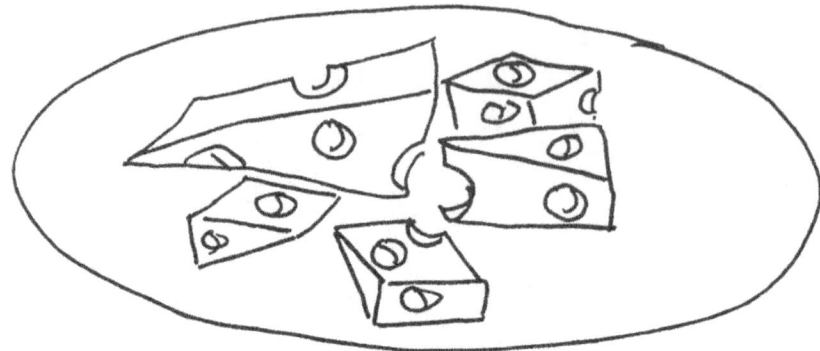

How many? _____

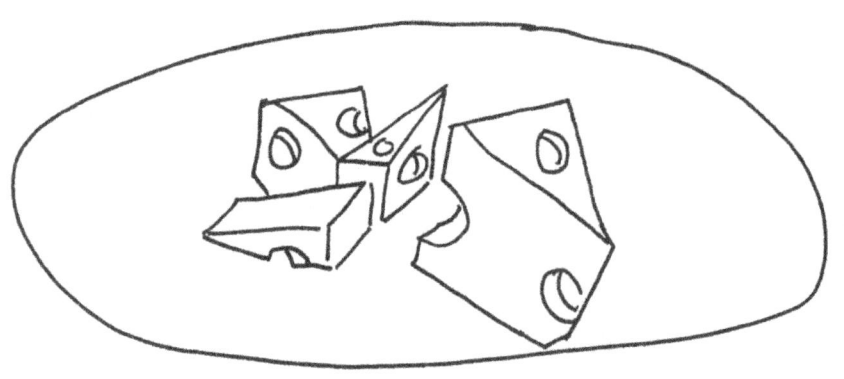

How many? _____

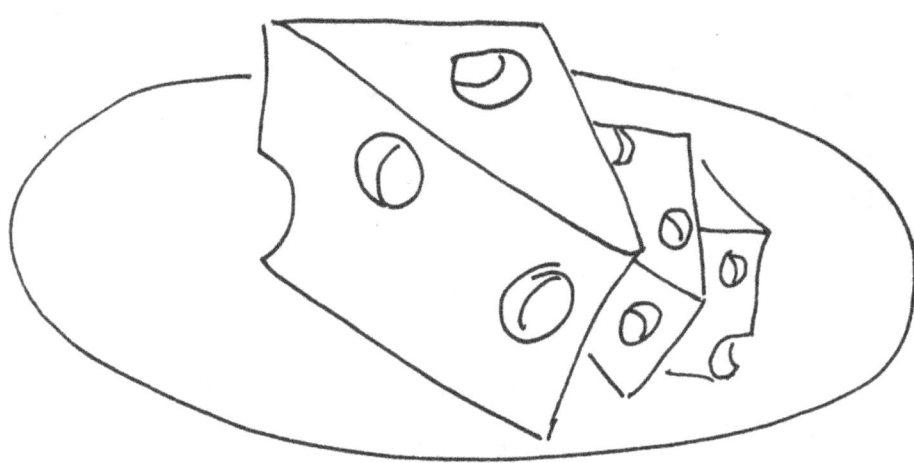

How many? _____

You are so much fun!

Find and circle all the things on Dr Casey's table that begin with the letter "C".

Use the Word Box to fill in the squares

Word Box
- House
- Mimi
- Oscar
- Keisha
- Javier
- Cheese

Picture clues:

Across

1.
4.
6.

Down

2.
3.
5.

Each of you are Special !

Everyone Loves Oscar!

Find and circle the
Onion, Cactus, Mail box, Rock, Ant, Sun, and Oscar.

CIRCLE all the letters you see.
Look for A, B, C, D, E, F, G, H, I, J, K and Z:

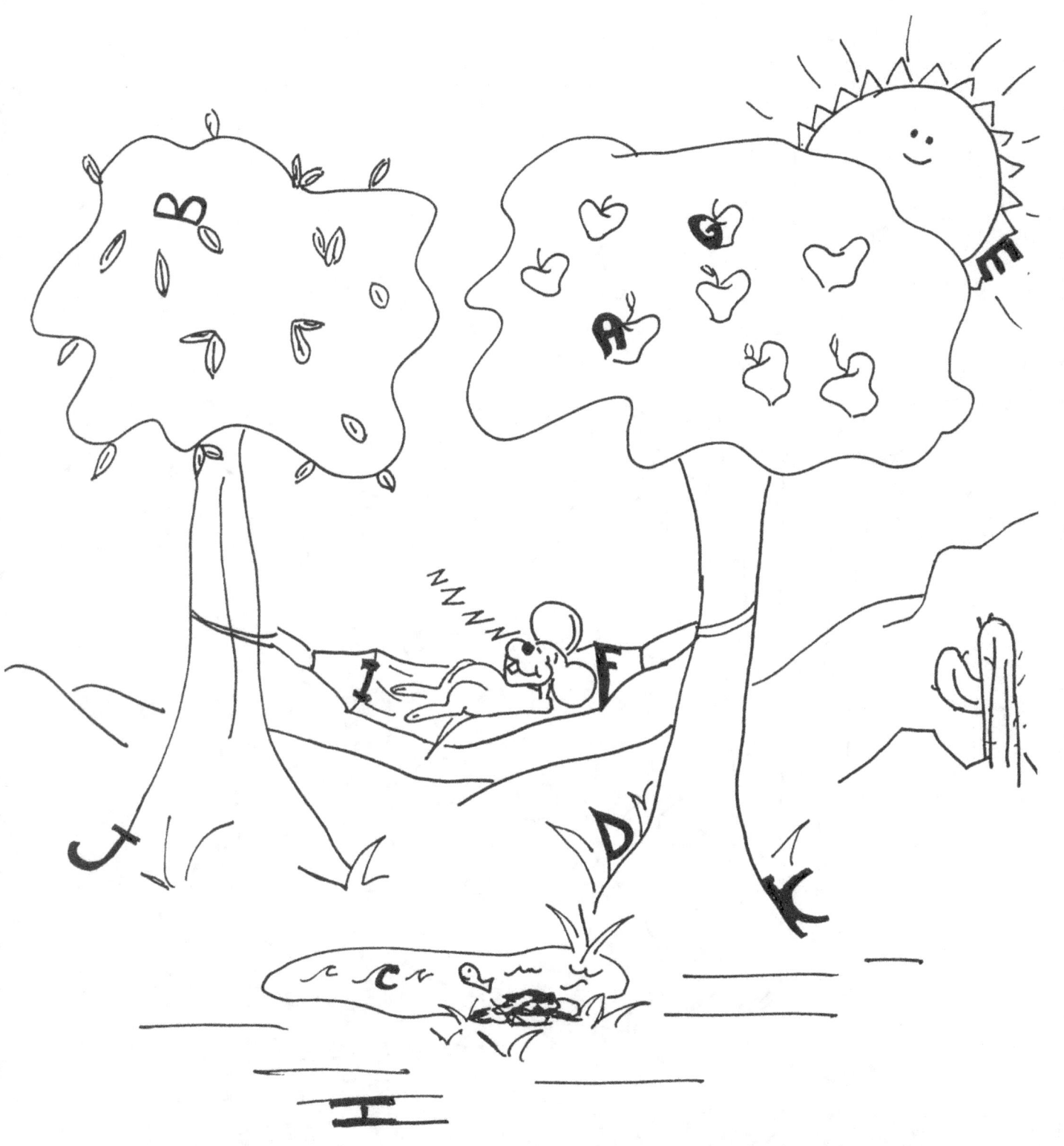

www.ingramcontent.com/pod-product-compliance
Lightning Source LLC
Chambersburg PA
CBHW081412070526
44583CB00020B/2779